THE MAN
WHO INVENTED THE
GAME OF BASKETBALL

The Genius of James Naismith

GENIUS INVENTORS AND THEIR GREAT IDEAS

Titles in the *Genius Inventors and Their Great Ideas* Series:

The Man Who Invented the Ferris Wheel: The Genius of George Ferris
Library Ed. ISBN: 978-0-7660-4136-3
Paperback ISBN: 978-1-4644-0206-7 • EPUB ISBN: 978-1-4645-1119-6
Single-User PDF ISBN: 978-1-4646-1119-3 • Multi-User PDF ISBN: 978-0-7660-5748-7

The Man Who Invented the Electric Guitar: The Genius of Les Paul
Library Ed. ISBN: 978-0-7660-4137-0
Paperback ISBN: 978-1-4644-0207-4 • EPUB ISBN: 978-1-4645-1120-2
Single-User PDF ISBN: 978-1-4646-1120-9 • Multi-User PDF ISBN: 978-0-7660-5749-4

The Man Who Invented the Laser: The Genius of Theodore H. Maiman
Library Ed. ISBN: 978-0-7660-4138-7
Paperback ISBN: 978-1-4644-0208-1 • EPUB ISBN: 978-1-4645-1121-9
Single-User PDF ISBN: 978-1-4646-1121-6 • Multi-User PDF ISBN: 978-0-7660-5750-0

The Man Who Invented Television: The Genius of Philo T. Farnsworth
Library Ed. ISBN: 978-0-7660-4139-4
Paperback ISBN: 978-1-4644-0209-8 • EPUB ISBN: 978-1-4645-1122-6
Single-User PDF ISBN: 978-1-4646-1122-3 • Multi-User PDF ISBN: 978-0-7660-5751-7

The Woman Who Invented the Thread That Stops Bullets: The Genius of Stephanie Kwolek
Library Ed. ISBN: 978-0-7660-4141-7
Paperback ISBN: 978-1-4644-0211-1 • EPUB ISBN: 978-1-4645-1124-0
Single-User PDF ISBN: 978-1-4646-1124-7 • Multi-User PDF ISBN: 978-0-7660-5753-1

The Man Who Invented the Game of Basketball: The Genius of James Naismith
Library Ed. ISBN: 978-0-7660-4142-4
Paperback ISBN: 978-1-4644-0212-8 • EPUB ISBN: 978-1-4645-1125-7
Single-User PDF ISBN: 978-1-4646-1125-4 • Multi-User PDF ISBN: 978-0-7660-5754-8

THE MAN WHO INVENTED THE GAME OF BASKETBALL

The Genius of James Naismith

Edwin Brit Wyckoff

Enslow Elementary

an imprint of

 Enslow Publishers, Inc.

40 Industrial Road
Box 398
Berkeley Heights, NJ 07922
USA

http://www.enslow.com

Content Advisors

Rachael Naismith
Assistant Director for Information and Research
Babson Library, Springfield College
(Birthplace of Basketball)®
Great-granddaughter of James Naismith

N.L. Zeysing
Historian
Naismith Memorial Basketball Hall of Fame
Springfield, Mass.

Series Literacy Consultant

Allan A. De Fina, Ph.D.
Past President of the New Jersey
Reading Association
Professor, Department of Literacy Education
New Jersey City University

Acknowledgment

The publisher thanks Springfield College in Springfield, Massachusetts, for its assistance in the publication of this book.

Enslow Elementary, an imprint of Enslow Publishers, Inc.
Enslow Elementary® is a registered trademark of Enslow Publishers, Inc.

Original edition published as *The Man Who Invented Basketball: James Naismith and His Amazing Game* in 2008.

Library of Congress Cataloging-in-Publication Data

Wyckoff, Edwin Brit.
  The man who invented basketball : the genius of James Naismith / Edwin Brit Wyckoff.
      p. cm. —(Genius inventors and their great ideas)
  Includes bibliographical references and index.
    ISBN 978-0-7660-4142-4 (alk. paper)
  1. Naismith, James, 1861-1939—Juvenile literature. 2. Basketball—United States—History—Juvenile literature. I. Title.
  GV884.N34W92 2012
  796.323092—dc23
  [B]

                                        2012013978

Future editions:
Paperback ISBN: 978-1-4644-0212-8
Single-User PDF ISBN: 978-0-7660-4142-4

EPUB ISBN: 978-1-4645-1125-7
Multi-User PDF ISBN: 978-0-7660-5754-8

Printed in the United States of America.
032013 Lake Book Manufacturing, Inc., Melrose Park, IL
10 9 8 7 6 5 4 3 2 1

To Our Readers: We have done our best to make sure all Internet addresses in this book were active and appropriate when we went to press. However, the author and the publisher have no control over and assume no liability for the material available on those Internet sites or on other Web sites they may link to. Any comments or suggestions can be sent by e-mail to comments@enslow.com or to the address on the back cover.

♻ Enslow Publishers, Inc., is committed to printing our books on recycled paper. The paper in every book contains 10% to 30% post-consumer waste (PCW). The cover board on the outside of each book contains 100% PCW. Our goal is to do our part to help young people and the environment too!

Photo Credits: Artville, p. 8; Courtesy of the Naismtih Museum, Almonte, Ontario, Canada, pp.12, 13, 16, 22, 25, 27, 29, 30, 31, 35; 1891 Football Team, International YMCA Training School (now Springfield College) Archives and Special Collections, Springfield College, Springfield Mass. p. 20; J.F. Patterson, Almonte, Ont., p. 9; McGill University Archives, Photograph Collection PL 007415 p.18; McGill University Archives, Photograph Collection PR 039193 p.19; Micheal Dunn, p.10; Shutterstock.com, pp. 8, 36, 39, 41, 42, 47; University Archives, Spencer Research Library, University of Kansas, p. 34.

Cover Photo: James Naismith: Kansas State Historical Society, Basketball players: Jupiter Images/Getty Images

CONTENTS

1 Tough Love and a Tough Life. 7

2 The Dropout. 14

3 The Preacher Plays Hardball 17

4 Inventing Fun. 24

5 The World Stood and Cheered 33

Timeline. 38

You Be the Inventor!. 39

Words to Know. 45

Learn More 46

Index. 48

Winters in Canada can be cold and harsh.

Chapter 1

Tough Love and a Tough Life

Winter in Canada can be very hard. Freezing wind sweeps down from the north. Rivers freeze solid. Crossing them can be scary and dangerous.

Young James Naismith

James Naismith turned eleven in 1872. He was old enough to know where the river near his home became safe, solid ice. But he took a shortcut he had never tried before. His team of horses pulled his wagon onto the frozen river. Their feet pounded the ice. Then one heavy hoof slammed through the sheet of ice. James jumped off the wagon and landed in the water. Grabbing the horses by their reins, he pulled hard. They were fighting him. Slowly he forced them through the broken ice to the other side of the river. They were so wet that icicles formed on the horses and the boy.

James grew up near Almonte, Ontario, in Canada.

This is the city of Almonte, Ontario, in Canada, as it looked in the early twentieth century.

James looked around. He saw his uncle Peter Young watching him from behind some trees. But his uncle had not helped. He wanted James to learn to solve problems by himself and not to take foolish chances. It was a tough lesson.

James had been born on November 6, 1861, near Almonte, Ontario, which is in Canada. When he was almost nine, his father, John Naismith, came down with deadly typhoid fever. It is very catching, so James, his sister, Annie, and brother, Robbie, were taken to their grandmother's home. A few days later their father died. Two weeks later, their mother, Margaret, died of the same disease. A short time later, their grandmother, Annie Young, died of old age.

After his parents died, James moved to this house, which belonged to his uncle Peter.

Their uncle Peter took care of them in a small village near Almonte called Bennie's Corners. It had a schoolhouse, a store, a blacksmith shop, and lots of other kids to play with. There was a swimming hole with a muddy hill for sliding right into the water. There were bunches of boys who loved wrestling, running, and high jumping. The children had lots of fun with very little money. When James needed ice skates, he made them. He took strips of old, rusty metal and sharpened them. He pounded the metal strips into wooden boards, and tied the boards to his shoes. Then he raced out onto the frozen swimming hole like a champion skater.

The best game in town was called duck on a rock. One player, the guard, would put a rock about the size of his fist on top of a great big rock near the blacksmith shop. The other boys threw stones at the "duck" to knock it off the big rock. If they missed, they had to pick up their stone before the guard could tag them. It sounds easy. It is not. The pitch could be soft, but it had to be perfectly aimed. When a player missed the duck, there was a lot of running, shouting, and laughing. James would remember duck on a rock years later when it was very important to him.

James and his friends used this big rock to play their favorite game, duck on a rock.

James (right) and his best friend, R. Tait MacKenzie, loved to spend time outdoors.

Chapter 2

The Dropout

James was great at sports. He also worked hard on the family farm. He did not work hard at school, though, and his grades were never very good. He wanted to grow up fast and be a man with a job. When he was fifteen, he left school and worked as a lumberjack. He cut down trees for almost five years. Then he decided to change his life.

James had a plan. He wanted to go back to high school and finish fast. His next step would be college. His sister and his uncle Peter wanted him to work on the farm. They argued. Finally they made a deal. James could go to college if he promised to study and become a minister after he graduated. He also promised to come home to work on the farm every summer. In 1883, James entered McGill University in Montreal, Canada.

One day when James was home for a visit, his brother, Robbie, had a terrible pain in his side. They all thought it was just a stomachache. It was actually a very bad infection right next to his stomach. Robbie died a few hours after the first stab of pain. A doctor could have helped him. The thought that Robbie could have been saved stayed in James's mind every day of his life.

In 1887, James graduated from McGill University after studying Hebrew and philosophy. Hebrew is an ancient language that many preachers study. Philosophy teaches people to think about life. James had a lot to think about.

James (front) won two sports awards at McGill University. Here he is with the gymnastics team.

Chapter 3

The Preacher Plays Hardball

For James, the next step was studying to become a minister at McGill's Presbyterian College. There was much to learn, and he studied day and night. His friends tried to get him to play sports. They told him it would sharpen his mind and toughen up his body. He said no and kept on studying.

One day his strong friends dragged him out to the football field. James had so much fun that he found time to study hard and play hard, too. He was smaller than the other players, but he was powerful and smart. He learned rugby, which is a very rough game. He loved lacrosse, which can be even rougher.

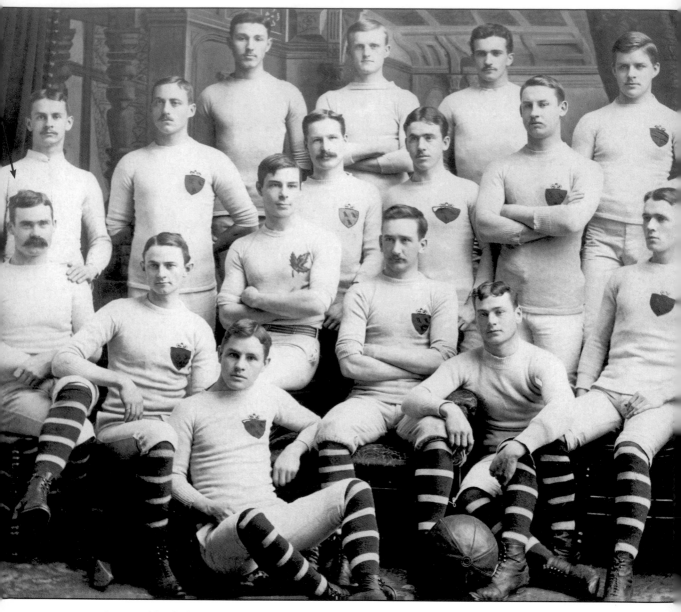

James (far left, seated) joined the rugby team at McGill University.

One Saturday James got two black eyes in a wild game of lacrosse. The next day was Sunday, and he had to give a sermon in the church. James, the student minister, looked out from behind those two black eyes. He may have looked kind of funny, but he finished the sermon he had written.

James Naismith as a young man

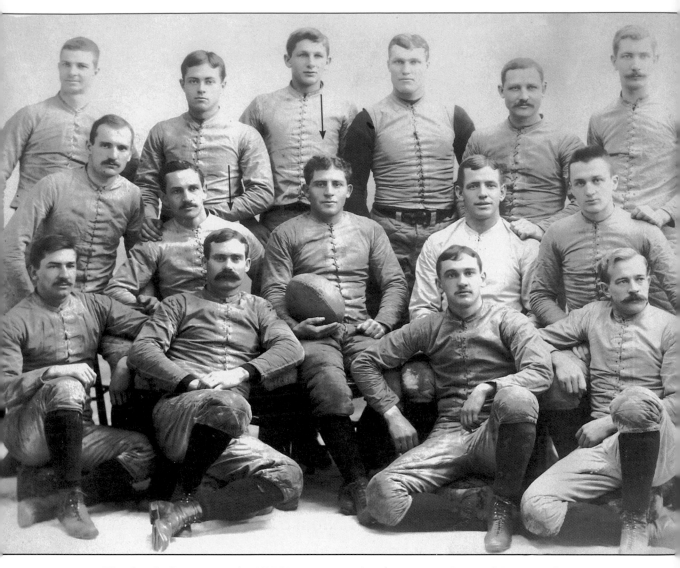

The football team at the YMCA training school poses in the uniforms used in games. Players in those days did not wear pads or helmets. James (front row, second from left) and Alonzo Stagg (center, with ball) became good friends.

McGill's football coach, Amos "Alonzo" Stagg, had been a famous football player at Yale University. He watched James smashing through the other teams' players. Stagg picked James for a very rough position on the team. He said, "Jim, I play you at center because you can do the meanest things in the most gentlemanly manner." Stagg admired the way James was rough and tough but never nasty.

In 1890, James became a Presbyterian minister, but he did not want to give sermons in a church. He thought he could help teens live better lives if he talked to them while teaching them sports. His sister and his uncle Peter were deeply disappointed. James was sorry, but he believed in his idea.

His first sports job was at the training college for the Young Men's Christian Association, or YMCA. He moved from Canada to Springfield, Massachusetts, in the United States. James was very good at the job of teaching baseball, field hockey, football, and rugby, which are great games

James (left) plays football with Stagg. James, who invented the football helmet, is wearing an early model.

during spring, summer, and fall. Winter was a problem. The men had to come indoors to exercise, which was not much fun. They were so bored that some of them wanted to quit the YMCA training college.

James was told to invent an exciting indoor game. It had to be ready in two weeks. That was the deadline.

Chapter 4

Inventing Fun

James struggled with the problem for twelve days. The game had to be fast and fun. It could not be risky, like football or rugby, with teams of men banging into the gym walls. James did not want people running with a ball. He did not want rough tackling. However, he did like the idea of throwing a ball at something. But throwing a ball hard indoors could be dangerous. That good old game from his childhood, duck on a rock, flashed into his head. He remembered how using a soft pitch was the best way to aim for the "duck." James's eyes lit up. He shouted out loud, "I've got it!"

There was no time to invent new equipment. Two peach baskets were used as goals. James explained the strange rules. Two teams of men dragged themselves onto the gym floor, grumbling. They took a soccer ball and started playing. The grumbling stopped. Cheers and shouts filled the gym. The date was December 21, 1891. Basketball was born.

Peach baskets were used as basketball goals before nets.

1. The ball may be thrown in any direction.
2. It can be batted with hands, but not with the fist.
3. No running with the ball.
4. Hold the ball only with the hands.
5. No holding, pushing, hitting, or tripping the other team's players.
6. Follow the rules or a foul will be declared.
7. Make three fouls and the other team is given a goal.
8. A goal is made when the ball goes into the basket.
9. When the ball goes out of bounds, the first person to touch it, or the umpire, will throw it onto the court.
10. The umpire is the judge of the players. He can call fouls.
11. The referee is the judge of the ball. He decides on goals.
12. Game time is two fifteen-minute halves.
13. The team with the most goals in that time is the winner.

James Naismith had invented the great game all by himself. He was crazy about sports. Basketball fascinated him. Even so, he was not interested in coaching. He just wanted people to play for fun. Soon teams formed in gyms all around town. Students in schools across the country began playing basketball. Women began playing, too.

Maude Sherman was on one of the first women's basketball teams.

A young woman named Maude Sherman was on one of the first women's teams. James and Maude became friends, then fell in love. They married on June 20, 1894. They would have five children together.

In a few years basketball started being played more like it is played today. The peach baskets changed to rope baskets. Backboards were added. Dribbling became popular because players were not allowed to hold the ball very long without throwing it. The ball bouncing off the floor as a player raced down the court sounded like a fast drumbeat. James thought dribbling was a great idea.

James and Maude moved to Denver, Colorado, in 1895. There James became director of physical education at the largest YMCA in the country. He was always working on his plan for the future. He remembered his brother dying horribly without help from a doctor. He had seen athletes have terrible accidents. He wanted to be a doctor and help people.

George L. Pierce invented the basketball used today.
Here is his sketch for the patent.

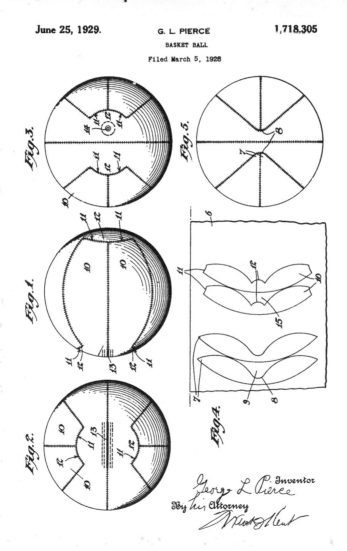

June 25, 1929.   G. L. PIERCE   1,718,305

BASKET BALL

Filed March 5, 1928

In 1892 baskets did not have a backboard.

James became a student at Gross Medical College, which was part of the University of Colorado in Denver. There was no stopping James when he had a plan. He worked all day at the YMCA and studied to be a doctor after work and on weekends. James graduated as a medical doctor in 1898.

James called this women's team, the Edmonton Commercial Grads, the finest example of a basketball team. They were world champions for seventeen years in a row.

His old friend Alonzo Stagg had become one of the most famous coaches in the whole country. Alonzo wanted James to work at the University of Kansas. He sent a telegram to the university: "Recommend James Naismith, inventor of basketball, medical doctor, Presbyterian minister, teetotaler, all-around athlete, non-smoker and owner of vocabulary without cuss words." The gentle man who had started basketballs bouncing around the whole wide world got the job of assistant physical director at the University of Kansas in 1898. By 1909 he was a professor, a preacher, and a medical doctor for the school.

Chapter 5

The World Stood and Cheered

In 1916, James became a minister in the United States Army. The next year, the YMCA sent him around the world to help American soldiers in World War 1. On May 5, 1925, the sixty-three-year-old Canadian became an American citizen.

In 1936, James was invited to the Olympic Games in Berlin, Germany. It was the first time basketball was an official game in the Olympics. Basketball teams were playing from countries all around the world. The players spoke different languages. They all wanted to shake hands with the inventor of basketball.

James Naismith could have made lots of money by selling sports equipment. He could have used his fame

James became the chaplain of the First Kansas Infantry during World War I.

working for companies that sell things like cigarettes. He refused the offers. He just wanted to do his job as a teacher, minister, and sports doctor.

By the time basketball was one hundred years old, millions of basketball fans were cheering their favorite teams and players. Hoops were hanging in many backyards. And street games were being played in cities all over the world.

The Philippines beat Mexico 32–30 in a second-round match at the 1936 Olympics. Mexico would go on to win the bronze medal, while the Philippines would make it to fifth place.

The game of basketball is James Naismith's enduring legacy.

James Naismith died suddenly on November 28, 1939. He was seventy-eight. He had been given a tough problem to solve. He invented a special kind of fun all by himself in just two weeks. He believed his sport could make the lives of young people better. And he was right.

TIMELINE

1861—Born on November 6, near Almonte, Ontario, Canada.

1870—Parents die; moves to village of Bennie's Corners, Ontario.

1887—Graduates from McGill University in Montreal, Quebec, Canada.

1890—Becomes a Presbyterian minister at McGill's Presbyterian College.

1891—Invents basketball at the YMCA training college in Springfield, Massachusetts; first game is played December 21.

1894—Marries Maude Sherman on June 20.

1895—Becomes director of physical education at YMCA in Denver, Colorado.

1898—Graduates as a medical doctor from Gross Medical College in Denver; becomes assistant physical director at the University of Kansas.

1909—Is professor, minister, and doctor at the University of Kansas.

1917—Helps American soldiers in World War I as a military chaplain.

1925—Becomes a United States citizen.

1936—Is honored at the Olympic Games in Berlin, Germany.

1939—Dies on November 28 of a heart attack at his home in Lawrence, Kansas.

YOU BE THE INVENTOR!

So you want to be an inventor? You can do it! First, you need a terrific idea.

Got a problem? No problem!

Many inventions begin when someone thinks of a great solution to a problem. One cold day in 1994, 10-year-old K.K. Gregory was building a snow fort. Soon, she had snow between her mittens and her coat sleeve. Her wrists were cold and wet. She found some scraps of fabric around the house, and used them to make a tube that would fit around her wrist. She cut a thumbhole in the tube to make a kind of

fingerless glove, and called it a "Wristie." Wearing mittens over her new invention, her wrists stayed nice and warm when she played outside. Today, the Wristie business is booming.

Now it's your turn. Maybe, like K.K. Gregory, you have an idea for something new that would make your life better or easier. Perhaps you can think of a way improve an everyday item. Twelve year-old Becky Schroeder became the youngest female ever to receive a U.S. patent after she invented a glow-in-the dark clipboard that allowed people to write in the dark. Do you like to play sports or board games? James Naismith, inspired by a game he used to play as a boy, invented a new game he called basketball.

Let your imagination run wild. You never know where it will take you.

Research it!

Okay, you have a terrific idea for an invention. Now what? First, you'll want to make sure that nobody else has thought of your idea. You wouldn't want to spend hours developing your new invention, only to find that someone else beat you to it. Google Patents can help you find out whether your idea is original.

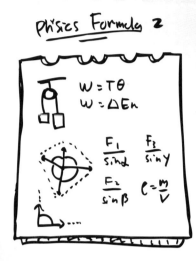

Bring it to life!

If no one else has thought of your idea, congratulations! Write it down in a logbook or journal. Write the date and your initials for every entry you make. If you file a patent for your invention later, this will help you prove that you were the first person to think of it. The most important thing about this logbook is that pages cannot be added or subtracted. You can buy a bound notebook at any office supply store.

Draw several different pictures of your invention in your logbook. Try sketching views from above, below, and to the side. Show how big each part of your invention should be.

Build a model. Don't be discouraged if it doesn't work at first. You may have to experiment with different designs and materials. That's part of the fun! Take pictures of everything, and tape them into your logbook.

Try your invention out on your friends and family. If they have any suggestions to make it better, build another model. Perfect your invention, and give it a clever name.

Patent it!

Do you want to sell your invention? You'll want to apply for a patent. Holding a patent to your invention means that no one else can make, use, or sell your invention in the U.S. without your permission. It prevents others from making money off of your idea. You will definitely need an adult to help you apply for a patent. It can be a complicated and expensive process. But if you think that people will want to buy your invention, it is well worth it.

WORDS TO KNOW

blacksmith—Someone who heats and hammers iron into different shapes like nails and horseshoes.

college—A school people go to after high school to study a certain subject, like math or writing.

dribbling—Bouncing a basketball off the floor.

minister—Someone whose job it is to talk to others about faith.

rugby—A team sport in which each player can kick, pass, or run with the ball, and tackle the other team's players.

sermon—A talk about faith, usually given by a minister in a church.

teetotaler—Someone who does not drink alcohol.

telegram—A message sent over a wire using Morse code. Telegrams were popular before many people had telephones.

typhoid fever—A deadly disease that can be caught from eating or drinking unclean food or water.

university—A school usually made up of more than one college.

LEARN MORE

Books

Hareas, John. *Basketball*. New York: DK Publishing, 2005.

LeBoutillier, Nate. *Play Basketball Like a Pro: Key Skills and Tips*. North Mankato, Minn.: Capstone Press, 2010.

Thomas, Keltie. *How Baseball Works*. Toronto: Maple Tree Press, 2005.

Triano, Jay. *Basketball Basics: How to Play Like the Pros*. Vancouver, Canada: Greystone Books, 2009.

Internet Addresses

To find out more about James Naismith and the game of basketball, check out these Web sites:

Naismith Museum
<www.naismithmuseum.com>

History of Basketball
<www.kansasheritage.org/people/naismith.html>

If you want to learn more about becoming an inventor, check out these Web sites:

Inventnow.org
<http://www.inventnow.org/>

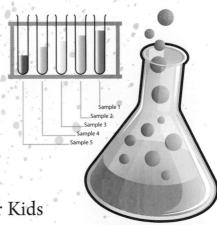

Inventive Kids
<http://www.inventivekids.com/>

The U.S. Patent and Trademark Office For Kids
<http://www.uspto.gov/kids/>

INDEX

A

Almonte, Ontario, 9

B

backboards, 28
basketball
  first ball design, 29
  first game, 25
  at the Olympics, 33
  original rules, 26
Bennie's Corners, Ontario, 11
Berlin, 33

D

Denver, Colorado, 28
doctor, 15, 28, 30, 32
dribbling, 28
duck on a rock, 11-12, 24

F

football, 17, 21, 24

G

Gross Medical College, 30

H

Hebrew language, 15

I

ice skates, 11
invent a game, 23, 24

L

lacrosse, 17, 19
lumberjack, 14

M

McGill University, 15, 17
minister, 14, 17, 19, 21, 32, 33

N

Naismith, Annie (sister), 10, 14, 21
Naismith, James
  American citizen, 33
  died, 37
  five children, 28
  married, 28
Naismith, John (father), 9
Naismith, Margaret (mother), 10
Naismith, Robbie (brother), 10, 15

O

Olympic Games, 33

P

peach baskets, 24, 28
philosophy, 15
Pierce, George L., 29
Presbyterian College, 17
professor, 32

R

rugby, 17, 21, 24

S

Sherman, Maude (wife), 28
Springfield, Massachusetts, 21
Stagg, Alonzo, 21, 32

U

University of Kansas, 32
U.S. Army, 33

W

women basketball players, 27

Y

YMCA, 21, 23, 28, 30, 33
Young, Annie (grandmother), 10
Young, Peter (uncle), 9, 11, 1 21